Shipping Container Homes

The Ultimate Guide To Building Shipping Container Homes For Sustainable Living, Including Plans, Tips, Cool Ideas, And More!

By: Anthony Hofman

Anthony Hofman

© Copyright 2016 - All rights reserved.

Table of Contents

Anthony Hofman

Introduction

The past few decades have welcomed a variety of innovative, unique, and sometimes quirky housing ideas. With the coming generations, the desire to live in a normal neighborhood or housing development has gone by the wayside. Even older generations are swapping out their same old, boring, single family homes for a more customized and exciting dwelling. Among this vast expanse of creative housing, there are several dwellings that prove to be the most popular. The tiny homes (either on wheels, converted sheds, etc.), converted motor homes and school buses, and storage container homes.

There is a significant amount of advantages when it comes to this new housing revolution. Individuals have the ability to customize and create a home anyway they see fit while in some cases, also being mobile. Not only that, some of these new types of homes are more environmentally friendly than the conventional homes.

One of these new types of homes that have caught the public eye and attention is the shipping container home. Yes, you heard right – homes made of shipping containers. At first, that may sound weird or even downright kooky. But in actual fact, shipping containers can be the ideal building material. This is because they are cuttable, movable, strong, stackable, durable, cheap and plentiful. Shipping containers are now so popular that they are not only used as homes but as stores, diners, offices, dormitories, schools, artists' studios, and even emergency shelters. Some people have even managed to use them as swimming pools!

This book is going to focus on storage container homes and everything it involves. I will examine what shipping container homes are in greater detail. I will also look at what the advantages and disadvantages of such a home are. I will give you information about where you can get shipping containers from, how to go about buying one and what are the most cost-effective methods of getting them. I will also tell you how you can plan and design your shipping container home and some alternative ways to use your shipping container.

It is my hope that by the time you finish reading this book, you will have a better understanding of shipping container homes and everything involved in building one.

Thank you for buying this book. I hope you have a good time going through it. I also hope that I give you all the information you need about this new and innovative style of housing.

Anthony Hofman

Chapter 1

What Are Shipping Container Homes?

Shipping container homes are just that; homes made from shipping containers. If you have ever driven by a warehouse or a port and observed large, rectangular metal boxes, you have seen a shipping container. These containers are used to transport items overseas and across countries to ensure that the contents of the container are immune to inclement weather, temperature, and other outside contaminants. Once these shipping containers reach their destination, they are either recycled, thrown away or sold to other companies to use for shipping.

Shipping containers have a lifespan of up to 30 years, but most companies quit using them around 10 years to avoid liability. Once these shipping containers are retired, as I stated before, they are recycled or sold to other individuals or businesses. One of the biggest questions surrounding shipping container homes is, well – how do you make a shipping container a home? Well, this depends on the buyer and the buyer's design. Some people choose to only use one shipping container as a home whereas some people use 10 or more – it really depends on your creativity and your budget.

Shipping container homes can be set down on a foundation and set side by side, making for a large, one story home whereas of individuals stack the containers on top of each other to create multistory dwellings. Each design comes with its own set of rules and regulations to ensure that your home is safe and durable, but we will go more in depth on that in the coming chapters.

Contrary to popular belief, there are different types of storage containers – some are more suitable for a residential dwelling than others. In fact, according to Shipping Containers Housing website, there are more than 50 different types of storage containers. This website also sites some of the more common shipping container types you will find:

Open Top: As the name implies, this container has a large opening at the top for loading materials in large quantities into them, such as grain or coal. The side of the container will also open up to make loading and unloading easier for heavy or taller, larger material.

Dry Freight: Also called "cube containers," they only open in the front. The rest of the container is completely sealed which is ideal for most general shipping needs.

Thermal/Insulated: Anything that needs to stay frozen or cold during shipping would go in this type of container. They are only insulated to maintain temperature; there is no external source of cooling.

Refrigeration: Also called reefer shipping containers, or reefers, these have the ability to be temperature controlled with built-in cooling systems for shipping perishable materials.

Tank: Used for shipping bulk or liquid materials, they have the same dimensions as rectangular containers, but are cylindrical in shape and mounted on a steel rectangular base.

All containers, regardless of characteristics or purposes, have dimensions that are regulated by the International Standards Organization (ISO). Standard height dimensions' range from 4 feet to 9.5 feet high, although the standard is 8.5 feet. Standard width is 8 feet, though some can vary based on use. Length is generally 20 feet or 40 feet, but some containers are as long as 56 feet.

Anthony Hofman

Chapter 2

How To Obtain A Shipping Container

There are a few different ways that you can obtain a shipping container. One of the most common ways is through the internet and the multiple resources available to purchase used shipping containers. A simple search for "used shipping containers" will supply you with more than enough resources to start with. There are several issues you may run into involving transport and shipping because shipping these containers can difficult to navigate if you are not shipping it locally. Often, before purchasing a shipping container, you may need to check the regulations in your area.

Some areas only allow shipping containers to reside at any residence or land for a certain amount of time without permits or the proper paperwork. This is especially the case if you intend to make a home out of your shipping container; check with your local state or county office to obtain more information on shipping containers and their regulations. Obtaining a shipping container needs to involve copious amounts of research on both ideas pertaining to the architecture and design of the home and the idea surrounding the placement of your home.

There are a lot of people who provide different tips and tricks on what to do before and during your shipping container search, some of which are incredibly helpful. An article by Mike Turber who wrote the article for a site called Offgridworld spoke of ten different things you need to keep in mind or do prior to buying a shipping container. According to Turber,

"1. Depending on where you live, buying a shipping container can be as easy as a trip to your local port or a logistical nightmare. If you live near a port, you should be able to find plenty of suppliers. If not, then you will need to have the container shipped to you. To save some money rent a truck with a tilting bed or a long tilting trailer and go pick it up yourself.

2. If you are on a budget, avoid any place that sells prefab containers with roll up doors or made to be contractor trailers used on work sites. These cost a lot, and you will probably need to change whatever layout they have to fit your own needs anyway.

3. Want to save money? Look for containers on Craigslist or even eBay. We were able to find a 40' HQ (High Cubed = 9.5' high) for $1,900. The average is about $2,200 for a 40HC,

$1,800 for a 20' and $1,500 for a 10'. One listing offered FREE delivery within a 50-mile radius, and the container came with a 3-year warranty to boot.

4. Want to save more money? Look around and check out some used containers. We visited a local warehouse that had several on their lot and was able to negotiate a 40' container down to just $500. Be careful though and make sure some shipping company does not own the container you are buying. This is easily determined by writing down the container number and calling the owner normally painted on the side.

6. Not all shipping containers are made from the same material. Look for those made from "Cor-Ten Steel." These will last the longest, and they will stand up to inclement weather and rust. Remember containers are designed to sit on a ship out in the corrosive salt air for years.

7. Negotiate with **ALL SELLERS!** This is extremely important. Do to the **HUGE** trade deficit with other countries, containers are piling up in the United States and other countries as well. The seller needs the space, and they are normally motivated to sell and make deals for multi-unit sales. Try to get **FREE** delivery.

8. Consider building the interior and alternate roof off site. Remember this is a big metal box and building prefabricated

sections and sliding them in or on at the last moment is an option. If not, you may be working in a hot or cold, hostile environment.

9. When you finish your home make certain that your insurance carrier knows it is an ISBU or Intermodal Steel Building Unit. It is most likely the outstanding fire and safety ratings that will impress insurance companies and code officials. In areas such as Florida or the coast of North and South Carolina that are more prone to hurricanes, these container houses offer a tremendous amount of sustainability and strength. Insurance companies know this and tend to encourage consumers to use them.

10. Here is a handy chart that will show you the dimensions and average cost. Note that the 40′ containers offer the best value and are by far the easiest to find. You can find sizes up to 53′ however it is our experience that the standard 40′ size or the 40'HC are the way to go."

Another great source for obtaining a shipping container as well as learning about the costs that these containers normally run is a website called "Shipping Container Housing." According to Shipping Container Housing, the cost of the shipping container homes is one of the greatest appeals to consumers. These can cost up to fifty percent less than the traditional construction of a new home and the biggest expense is the purchase of the actual container itself.

The cost of any given shipping container is variable under many conditions. Age, conditions, market value, and locating are just a few of them. Because of the variety of types of containers available, it is difficult to set a specific price as you would for other retail items. However, there are guidelines for determining prices.

Because of the resources needed to transport these containers, location is going to be a major factor. The further you are located (or the container's final destination) is from any shipping port or depot is going to rack up a great deal of expense. Your best bet in this situation is to contact the manufacturer directly to arrange transport of your container through them.

As we have mentioned before, if your container's final destination is not located near a readily available supply of containers, your shipping costs will be a major factor to consider. Also note that the more remote the destination, the more complicated the entire process will be, also resulting in an increase in pricing. Your best option is to find containers that are close to you, which will require some time. Wanting to create a shipping container home for yourself is a balancing act – if you invest time, even years, in searching out the best option, you may save yourself some serious money. If you are not willing to or do not have the time to spend years looking, expect to spend more money on your endeavor.

A good way to estimate shipping costs is to use an online freight shipping calculator. For example, to ship a 40-foot container from Jacksonville, Florida to Atlanta, Georgia, it might cost around $500. There will be other variables to account for that the calculator will not allow as input but it will give you a baseline to budget your project around.

Because market conditions also play a vital role in pricing, you may find less expensive containers farther away from where you are located. Just like stocks or any in-demand product, the prices will vary greatly in different regions. Spending time studying the shipping container market will pay off greatly in terms of saving yourself money in the long run. Become familiar with what's out there, what's in demand and what you want, which will allow you to make a better decision that suits your needs.

The condition of your desired container is also going to play a part in the overall cost. For purposes of this book, we will only focus on the containers that are going to be suitable for converting into livable spaces. A used 20-foot container will cost between $1400 -$2000, while a brand new one is going to be around $3200. For a 40-foot container, a used one should cost around $1600-$2700, while a new one will be upwards of $4500 to $5000. Keep in mind these estimates are for the container only. The price of shipping is not included and will vary based on size and other conditions mentioned above.

It will be helpful to understand some of the terms used to describe shipping containers so you know exactly what you are getting. An ideal option will be a "one trip" container. These generally have only been used once to ship freight, and are as close to new as you will find, but they will still be on the higher end of the used price spectrum.

Aside from a one trip container, others may have been used for many years in shipping. While most are structurally sound there will be significantly more wear and tear than with a one trip container. These might be a good choice if you are looking to build additional structures and want to keep your cost low, however they may not be suitable to choose for your primary residential structure.

Containers that have been "retired" are sometimes called WWT containers. They are deemed as no longer worthy of shipping freight anymore, and they have been put out in a yard, basically just sitting stagnant. They are, however, still suitable for protection against the elements. These might not be the best option for a living quarter, but they can still serve a purpose as a storage container. You should have no problems finding wind and water sealed containers in large port areas.

When it comes to a container listed "as-is," you should not take that condition listing lightly. These types of containers are deserving of a thorough look through by someone who is familiar with shipping containers and their faults. Be aware, too, that some sellers list containers "as-is" to protect themselves from any claims the buyer may make against them, and the container may be in excellent condition. Even if the container appears to be in perfect condition, as-is containers should be approached with caution. As far as the cost is concerned, these will be on the lower end and should be significantly discounted as a result of their wear and tear.

As with literally everything that gets used, the older it is the more use it will have had, resulting in tougher wear on the item. Used containers might not be the best choice for building a shipping container home, unless you have found a rare gem in the used market that is in flawless condition. If you are interested in a shipping container home, but fairly new to the idea, a good place to start would be with a shipping container shed or storage space. The cost associated will be much less and it will give you an idea of internal construction, space, and capacity. Because an older container would be suitable for this, you get a "practice run" in with container maintenance.

You might be surprised at the availability of shipping containers. Websites that list miscellaneous items, such as Craigslist, train stations, and local papers are good places to start your search. Especially if you are near a port city or within a reasonable distance from the coast, they will be incredibly easier to find and most likely a little on the cheaper side. Shipping container auctions are also a good route to find used containers, and this usually gives you an opportunity to inspect the container before you begin bidding on it. A simple internet search will yield many results on used shipping containers, from companies solely dedicated to selling containers to general auction sites, such as eBay. These sites will also give you insight into competitive rates and other market information.

Shipping Container Companies are a good way to go if you want new or one trip containers that for the most part are appropriate for use with ship container homes. Some companies include:

- BSL Containers

- Containerhouse International, Inc.

- W&K Container

- Rava Group Container Services

The Shipping Containers Housing website also describes companies that exist exclusively for building shipping container homes for you, alleviating you from the struggle of starting at square one with an empty container. There are many reasons to consider using an established company to do the work for you.

The first reason for using a company established for this type of project is outright convenience. Not only can building inside of the container be a hassle, but companies with prefabricated domiciles have also taken into account any jurisdictional red tape you might encounter when it comes to building codes and permits, as some areas may not have or may be unfamiliar with container housing construction. Reputable and well-established companies familiar with ISO containers have technical knowledge about the building process, as well as expertise in ushering your project through the legal process of obtaining permits and approvals.

Construction of a shipping container home is not an easy endeavor to undertake, just as building a traditional home would not be if you were unfamiliar with that process. If you are interested in building a cabin, shed, or workshop, these will be much easier DIY projects than building an entire living area. You can typically use one container for smaller projects since they will be used occasionally rather than serving the purpose of being lived in. Building a smaller area like a workshop or cabin will give you some experience in the realm of shipping container building which you can later apply to building your own home.

Bear in mind that not all "small" projects are good starting points. For instance, constructing a bunker is not recommended as a starter project when it comes to converting a shipping container. Bunkers require complex reinforcements to be effective, making it a daunting DIY project. Bunkers are also partially or completely buried underground, adding to the rigor of DIY construction.

If you are looking to construct a dream home out of a shipping container, then there are definitely advantages to using a company that specifically builds shipping container homes. They will be experienced with the entire process, planning, designing, and anticipating issues you may encounter along the way with any part of the process. There are several companies out there that have experience in building luxury homes out of steel containers.

Do not assume that hiring a company to do the job for you will leave you out of the process. It is your home, and your involvement is almost mandatory. Even with normal home construction and contractors that build custom homes, the customer will tell you that it took a lot of time and thought to construct their dream. Since you will be the one living there, you want to be involved in the process to make sure very little detail makes it feel like home to you.

If you are looking for a simpler process, there are prefabricated container homes available. The basic necessities of a container home are already built and the room sizes are pre-planned, floor layouts are completed and other basics. Many times, features such as light fixtures, trim, countertops, etc. can be chosen by the customer, but buying prefab will alleviate the stresses of starting with an empty container.

If you seek a middle ground between an empty container and a complete prefab house, another benefit to using a company that specializes in such construction is the availability of various floor plans. You can have them build exactly what is drawn up on the blueprint or alter the plans to suit your needs. Based on the size of your container, they will already have floor plans that accommodate the available space which allows you to see the layout of your new home.

An added bonus to using a container home builder is that they have experience in building the floor plans they offer. If they've built your chosen floor plan a few times before, they will already be familiar with materials and plans needed. This allows them to foresee issues that might arise during the building process, since the chances are that they have already constructed a type that you've selected.

A container kit is one option for the DIY shipping container home enthusiast that does not have much experience in building with cargo containers. As with any project, to begin a DIY adventure, it is always easier to start with a kit that comes with instructions and guidance rather than attempting to build something from scratch. When purchasing a container home kit, they provide instructions and support for each step of the project.

Finding a shipping container home construction company can be very time consuming and take a lot of investigation on your part. There are a few exemplary companies that provide different levels of services, from planning and design to already prefabricated homes that are ready to live in. Addis Containers, based out of New Zealand, is a shipping container design and construction company that offers several plans that they can customize to suit your needs.

MEKA World is a good example of a container housing company. MEKA not only provides attractive container homes that are sure to suit anyone, but they also offer larger multifamily projects for families that need more room. They offer containers that range in size from 320 square feet up to 1920 square feet.

Logical Homes is another company worth looking in to. The have developed container homes that are "impressive, and some are downright incredible," according to the Shipping Container Housing website.

Adam Kalkin, of Kalkin & Co., is an architect that offers a couple different kinds of shipping container projects. The Quick House is a completely prefabricated home kit, constructed from recycled shipping containers. It offers 3 bedrooms and 2 ½ baths in its 2000 square foot model. They also manufacture 1000, 3000, and 5000 square foot models of the Quick House.

They also offer the $99,000 House. It consists of a dual structure made from a modified shipping container and a prefabricated steel structure. Although this option is not 100% made from a shipping container alone, it demonstrates the possibilities available if you are willing to expand the type of construction for your container home.

As you may have already grasped, obtaining a shipping container home requires taking in a lot of different facets while also doing a significant amount of research to make sure you shop smart and efficiently.

Chapter 3

Risks Involved With Shipping Container Homes

Despite a large amount of advantages to owning a shipping container home, there is also a lot of disadvantages. Although people believe that a shipping container home is significantly cheaper than other forms of dwellings, depending on the type of shipping container home you are looking for, this could not be further from the truth. In some cases, these types of homes are cheaper than modern residences. If you are looking to add multiple shipping containers on top of one another, you are going to need to add additional expenses.

These expenses can range from insulation costs, HVAC systems, foundation building, reinforcements to ensure the containers do not collapse after years of use. Shipping containers generally are only safe for inhabitation for around 30 years and after that, they can begin to rust and break down, creating a dangerous environment over time. Shipping containers also do not come with anything inside of them, meaning you are responsible for all the interior add-ins such as plumbing, doors, windows, counter tops – everything.

There is also a risk when purchasing a storage container that the container was transporting hazardous chemicals. If it important to do your research prior to purchasing the container because, should you purchase a container than houses toxic chemicals for several years, it is going to be next too impossible to completely eliminate and risk of harmful effects on your body. Shipping containers, although seemingly easy to clean, unfortunately a simple wipe down and even pressure washing is not enough to rid the entire unit of certain harmful chemicals.

Some storage containers also ship items that are heavier than other containers so even though your container may only be 5-10 years old, the wear and tear on it might have aged the container far beyond its years – similar to a car. One of the best ways to avoid this is to inquire further into the business you are purchasing from and see if anyone has purchased containers from them in the past for the purpose of creating a residential unit. Certain companies that have a large residential customer base might be the best companies to purchase from because their containers are more reliable than others.

I cannot stress enough the importance of doing your research when it comes to purchasing a shipping container as a residential dwelling. Once you have purchased the unit, very rarely is it refundable so choose wisely and preferably by a referral so you have some idea of what to expect from the company. If you are looking to purchase a shipping container for a home, as I stated previously, there is going to be nothing in the unit initially so if your idea is to save money, sometimes shipping containers warrant the spending of additional money to get the home you desire especially if you are using more than one shipping container. You are essentially buying the shell of your home so it is up to you to too build the inside. This can be seen as a disadvantage for anyone who is unfamiliar with home improvement and architecture because this could mean you need to rely on an outside source or contractor to build and design the inside of your home which would cost even more.

There is a great article on a website called Container Home Plans. This website goes over the potential risks of owning and residing in a container home. According to the website, a question that is most frequently asked by people is whether or not the shipping containers contain any harmful or toxic chemicals. An article published in the *Arch Daily* by Brian Pagnotta illustrated the pros and cons of living in a shipping container home. If you've never read the article, it is worth a read if you are considering building your own container home. He points out two main concerns concerning harmful chemicals in your new home. Firstly, container homes that use wood floors usually have been treated with pesticides to keep pests out of your home and from destroying the floors. Secondly, some paints used to paint shipping containers have chromate and phosphorus in them.

This is not an end all, be all situation though. Brian is right in raising the concerns of chemicals in your home, but bear in mind that if you are purchasing from a container home construction company, you can specify to the builder that you do not want your floors treated and you do not want specific coatings or paints in your new home. The flip side of this is that your cost will increase drastically, since you will be buying a brand new container. You also lose out on the environmentally friendly aspect of not using a recycled container.

Now arises the issue in using secondhand containers. Regardless of what the container was used for or what it was used to ship, chances are it has been treated with various chemicals to resist whatever was being shipped in it, weather, moisture, or pests. To find out, you will need to do some investigating. You can contact the original manufacturer of the container to find out if it was treated with anything hazardous. Each container has unique identification number you can find to find out who made the container.

If the container comes with flooring that has already been installed and it has been treated with chemicals you prefer not be in your home, you still have options. Larry from Sea Container Cabin converted used shipping containers in 2010. To protect himself from the chemicals used in the flooring, he used a non-breathable underlayment. If this does not suit your comfort level with chemicals, you could always remove the flooring and install marine plywood for your flooring, which is available at most hardware stores.

Flooring chemicals in just one issue associated with using a recycled, used shipping container. Many containers that are shipped via boat across the ocean are coated with a chemical to protect it from saltwater as it travels. It is a practical expense for manufacturers because they need to be sure the cargo inside the containers is protected during shipping. However, it is not very desirable to someone looking to use this container as a new home. Your first step is to contact the manufacturer to find out exactly what chemicals have been used on the container.

Your best option for containers that may have been previously treated with toxic chemicals is to use an insulation that comes as a foam spray. You will need to spray the entire interior of the container, which will create a vapor barrier that will resist any fumes from the chemicals seeping into your new home.

There are also concerns from people who live in natural disaster prone areas about whether or not a shipping container home can withstand the forces of a hurricane. After Katrina, there were many photos showing traditional wooden homes that had been obliterated by the hurricane. In the midst of the debris there were completely intact shipping containers.

When used as shipping containers, they are built to withstand being stacked on top of one another, nine high, each fully loaded with cargo up to 26 tons per container. With that in mind, it is no wonder these containers stood up to the destructive forces of Hurricane Katrina. After the disaster, a relative boom in the use of shipping containers as emergency disaster shelters occurred.

The most well-known area for this is in New York. In April 2014, Bill de Blasio, the Mayor of New York City, announced the creation of the Post-Disaster Housing Prototype Program. The structure that upheld itself as the strongest option was the shipping container home.

New York is aiming to use shipping containers to create stackable apartments that can be used after a natural disaster occurs. Since these containers are stackable, it makes them an ideal choice for densely populated areas. There is not much evidence to show that a shipping container home has actually faced the forces of a hurricane, but we do know that the containers themselves have been through such disasters.

In Graceville Container House: Case Study, Todd Miller built a container home using 31 total containers. The entire structure was placed on micro-pile foundations nine meters deep and capped off with piers made of concrete. The containers were then anchored down and secured on the top of the piers. His house was featured on "Grand Designs Australia," where he made the claim that his house cyclone proof because of the foundational and anchoring methods used for his home. Another interested note about Todd's home is that he constructed it in an area of known flood planes in Queensland. According to Todd's building plans, they also showed that his container home was essentially able to withstand a flood, when the local building authorities approved his plans.

Another concern about shipping container homes is the level of security they provide. Typically, it appears that the people concerned with this issue are looking into building a cabin or cottage. They want to be able to leave their container unattended for weeks or months on end without worrying about someone breaking into it or moving themselves right in to the dwelling.

Are shipping container homes secure? I have received this question a surprising amount of times. When I've dug a bit deeper and asked questions back, the people who tend to ask, 'are they secure', are those who are planning on using them as a cabin in the elements of nature. When using the container for this reason, they want to be able to leave their home for months at a time without having to worry about someone breaking into it.

For an understanding of the built-in security measures for your shipping container home, let's get back to the basics of what shipping containers are designed for. In the 1950s with the use of the first shipping containers, the amount of 'lost' (or stolen) cargo dropped significantly. Before their utilization, goods were loaded onto ships in crates, barrels, or sacks – known as break bulk cargo – none of which are secure at all. Laborers on these ships were known to steal goods, and it was simply considered to be the "price of shipping." Shipping containers are designed to be airtight and impenetrable to safely ship miscellaneous cargo and goods around the world. Since shippers now had the ability to lock the containers before it even got to the shipping port, the reduction in stolen goods was dramatically decreased. Simply stated, shipping containers are one of the most secure structures available when it comes to default security.

However, it should be noted that when people begin to convert shipping containers into livable spaces, they tend to cut into the original structure of the container, jeopardizing the innate security of the structure. For a building like a cabin or a cottage, something that will spend time being unattended to, it is recommended that you put any windows or doors behind the original shipping container doors.

By leaving the external structure intact, you can be sure that when you lock those original doors, the structure will be secured from anyone trying to break in. Then, when you are using your cabin, you can prop open the doors of the shipping container and open up your installed windows and doors for light and easy access while you are there.

This article has attracted thousands of people in search of information regarding the risks of owning a shipping container home. There is no such thing as too much browsing or too much research when it comes to learning about shipping container homes. You would not purchase a house without first looking into the potential risks vs reward which is why you should not treat a shipping container home any less than you would a normal home. It may be different, unique, and maybe even slightly extreme but it is still a home and it is where you will sleep, eat, and drink – do not you want to know you are safe?

Arch Daily is another great source for learning about the possible negative sides of owning or purchasing a shipping container for living in. Arch Daily actually believes that using a shipping container as a residential dwelling is not the greatest idea, regardless of the advantages people claim they have. Arch Daily states, "What's wrong with shipping container buildings? Nothing, if they're used for the right purpose. For a temporary facility, where an owner desires the shipping container aesthetic, they can be a good fit (look, I've even done a container project!). For sites where on-site construction is not feasible or desirable, fitting a container out in the factory can be a sensible option, even though you'll still have to do things like pour foundations on site. It probably will not save you any money over conventional construction (and very well might cost more), but it can solve some other problems.

The place where containers really do not make any sense is housing. I know you've seen all the proposals, often done with a humanitarian angle (building slum housing, housing for refugees, etc.) that promise a factory-built "solution" to the housing "problem" but often positioned as a luxury product as well."

The article continues to articulate why it is a bad idea to consider a shipping container for a home, stating that housing is not a technology problem. For the most part, buildings and homes anywhere in the world have been built appropriately for the local region. Sometimes there are material shortages. Sometimes there are situations when a factory-built structure is needed – such as during the aftermath of a natural disaster – but it should not be containers that are used.

The article questions why anyone would want to live a container that is only 7 feet inside, and by the time you insulate and construct the walls, you are left with building code minimums as habitable space. It does not seem ideal, and shipping wider structures is certainly possible since modular home builders do it all the time.

Insulation is another issue. It requires that walls are built either inside or outside of the container. Building them inside allows for space for electrical and plumbing components, but will cut down on the living space in the container. If you try to insulate the container on the outside, it will no longer have the appearance of a container. On top of that, you will then have to build walls around the insulation to protect it – just as any other house would have. In either case, you are forced to duplicate the walls of the original structure. If insulating from the inside is done improperly, it can cause condensation to build up against the metal walls of the container.

The structure of a shipping container as a home also poses other problems. The containers are designed with steel beams as a frame, and the walls of it are actually a very thin gauge steel. This is because of the way the containers are designed to be stacked on top of one another. As soon as you start constructing inner walls inside the container, for the best and strongest structure to result, you need to add steel beam reinforcements to everything. If you cut openings in the sides of the container, you begin to inhibit the integrity of its construction, making the frame beams useless. The steel reinforcing is extremely expensive but absolutely necessary to combine containers to create a "double wide."

In cases where containers are being considered as apartment buildings, it is impractical to do so. In a recent competition, it was mentioned that because containers can be stacked nine-high, concrete floors could be utilized every nine floors. This does not really save on construction costs for a couple of reasons. Firstly, the bottom of the stack needs to be able to support the entirety of the weight above it. Adding concrete only increases the weight on the base, requiring the need for reinforcements. Secondly, if building up, the entire structure would require a traditional foundation, which is one of the most expensive parts of a building project. The idea of stacking also requires a lot of room and large equipment. The large crane and safety regulations required to operate it, along with the staging site needed for all of the containers, would be almost nightmarish in a densely populated urban setting.

Then the container presents issues with mechanical systems and utilities in the house. Because of issues with insulating the container already mentioned, you will need a very high-functioning HVAC system to regulate the temperature inside the container. There is only so much you can do to maintain aesthetics while turning a shipping container into a habitable home. Even the tallest containers are only 9.5 feet tall, and by the time you run ducts and wiring through, you significantly cut down on the living height within the structure.

The article also touches upon the idea of using recycled containers and the somewhat misconceived notion that is a "green" idea. It is somewhat true that there is a surplus of containers that are not being used, just sitting around taking up real estate. Used containers need to be thoroughly cleaned and checked for hazardous chemicals, either used in manufacturing the container itself or possibly residue remaining from whatever was shipped in any given container.

Anthony Hofman

Chapter 4
Stories Of Success

Locals to Arizona are not unfamiliar to the latest shipping container fad. With so many of them battling to find affordable housing, shipping container homes offer a not only affordable option but also a decent living space. According to an article in Tween Tribune, an old stack of shipping containers resting in an industrial section of Phoenix has some developers rethinking what it means to construct a livable building. This stack has been converted into eight apartments. Shipping company logos, serial numbers, and scuff marks remain on the outside, but on the inside of each one, you will find a 740 square foot modern home. According to Patrick Tupas, a member of the United States Air Force, "It does not even feel like a shipping container. It is also insulated really well. It just feels like a regular apartment." He and his wife have signed a one-year lease on one of these apartments for $1000 per month rent.

"In a stack of shipping containers sitting in a lot in an industrial section of Phoenix has some developers thinking inside the box. The structures usually used to transport cargo have been transformed into eight apartments. Scuff marks, old serial numbers, and shipping company logos remain. But a look inside each unit reveals a 740-square-foot modern home. "It does not even feel like a shipping container. It is also insulated really well," said Patrick Tupas. He is in the Air Force and along with his wife signed a one-year lease for $1,000 a month. "It just feels like a regular apartment."

He continued to explain that was a downside to living in a shipping container. People passing by ask him questions about living in there and press him to see inside, clearly not believing how someone could live in such a seemingly small space. Container projects have begun to spring up in Washington, Detroit, and Las Vegas for housing or retail spaces. It is referred to as "cargotecture" and developers are working to find a way to fill the generational gap between baby boomers and millennials who want to live closer to larger cities with all they have to offer.

Dana Cuff, director of cityLAB at UCLA, states "They are faster, cheaper and now potentially have much more of an aesthetic range." CityLAB studies urban growth and architecture and says that some companies will try to hide the origins and uses of shipping containers, but not in Phoenix. The developer in

Phoenix, Stark James, calls the project Containers on Grand, and they have designed the apartments in such a way that they were able to maintain the corrugated metal exteriors. Each apartment is actually two containers, and inside shows no evidence that they were once used to transport cargo.

The interior walls are painted white, and the original flooring has been encased in epoxy. There are a bedroom and a living room for the two main areas, connected by two hallways. One hallway contains the kitchen area with an oven, and the other hallway has a nook and a closet. There is also room for a washer/dryer unit. In Phoenix, all but two of the apartments are rented out, and one is being marketed as a vacation rental.

Since 2004, in Washington's Brookland neighborhood, a four-story housing unit has been occupied by young professionals and college students. In Las Vegas, there is a retail complex consisting of the use of shipping containers. Three Squared Construction in Detroit has in the works $14 million worth of projects, utilizing shipping containers as the basis because using them saves time. As of April 2015, Detroit opened its first residential shipping-container development project.

The CEO of Three Squared Construction, Leslie Horn, says there is a high demand for these apartments from empty nesters and millennials. The three story building periodically rents out the top floor, showcasing the structure. Horn said they only save about five percent in the cost of lumber, but the time saved is where the advantage really adds up, because the entire "building" can be constructed faster.

Stark James, based out of Scottsdale, Arizona, is working on constructing twelve more container homes in Phoenix, stacked three high. Because container home manufacturing is seen by others in the industry as non-conventional, architect Brian Stark says they receive a lot of teasing from other companies that they work with. The downtown Phoenix development will be called "The Oscar" after Oscar the Grouch – this is a humorous play on the question Brian says they get asked most often, "How are the garbage can homes going?"

Chapter 5
Benefits To Shipping Container Homes

Like disadvantages, there are a lot of advantages to owning a shipping container home. According to a well-known site called "Shipping Container Homes," this site explains that, "While shipping containers are constructed to be used again and again, many eventually fall into disuse and end up sitting around the ports in China, northern Europe and the United States."

Reports suggest that at any given moment on the planet, there are an estimated 17 to 20 million ISO containers sprinkled around the world at any given time, with as many as one million of them sitting around taking up space. Depending on its use, a shipping container can have many names, unofficially and officially. When used solely for the purpose of shipping cargo, they may be called:

- ISO Container (ISO stands for International Standards Organization)

- Cargo container

- Conex box

- Ship container

- Sea container

- Shipping crate

- Steel container

- Storage container

When the containers are used for building, you may hear them referred to as:

- ISBU (Intermodal Steel Building Unit)

- ISBU module

- GreenCube

On the Shipping Container Housing website, many of the terms are used interchangeably. In a professional sense, it will be rare that you will find anyone calling houses made this way "shipping crate homes," but it is still a correct account of the building.

Since 2004, and even more so since 2010, the shipping container home building project has taken a giant trending leap upward. Creative companies and even individuals see the potential in repurposing containers that are just sitting around, clogging up space and the environment, and turn them into aesthetically pleasing and practical domiciles.

There are countries all over the world that have taken this project and ran with it. Just to name a few where the idea seems to be trending, included are the United States, United Kingdom, Poland, the Netherlands, Chili, Canada, South Africa, Spain, Estonia, Switzerland, Norway, Australia, and New Zealand.

Not only does this type of dwelling appeal to environmentally conscious crowds because of its eco-friendly nature, but there are other advantages to point out according to CBS News and Popular Mechanics:

- Repurposing of unused containers scattered around the world's shores.

- Relatively economical investment, costing between $1000 and $2000 each.

- Being made from galvanized steel makes them stronger and more durable than typical wood-framed housing.

- Because the main structure is already in place, pre-built homes have been assembled in a little as three days.

- Because of the basic rectangular shape, it allows for easy design plans.

- There is an ability to place containers side-by-side or stack them for more room.

- Construction on the interior can be completed anywhere, then it can be transported to its final destination.

- Materials age well and require little maintenance.

- They can be resistant to termites, fire, and mold.

- When building a house with shipping containers homes can be modified later on to include new modules

Not all shipping containers are created equal. You have several types from which to choose, each with different characteristics and costs. Grabbing a container and calling it a day will not take you very far, either, as you still need the know-how and amendments to transform the container from a cargo carrier to your home sweet home.

Regardless of whether you plan to create a quaint, simple home or a glamorous "mansion" of sorts, in terms of the overall cost to build a shipping container home versus a standard home, the shipping container option will cost significantly less. According to Bob Vila's website, the cost per square foot of a shipping container home is about half that of a traditional structure home. This is of course dependent on a few factors, such as the amount of decoration and design you desire, and the company you hire to do the construction. For the most part though, shipping container homes cost much less than traditional home-building projects, so it is no wonder the trend is on the rise.

Not to be neglected is the installation of utilities – water and electricity – and other comforts of home. Contractors for these areas can cost anywhere from $75 to $150 per hour, not including materials. Also keep in mind the cost of land to place your new home and any permits you will need to secure to ensure your shipping container home fits within the guidelines of local laws and regulations.

One final thing to remember is that you are going to get a lot of attention from others about your choice of dwelling. You will become part of an eco-friendly trend that is economical and even a little cool, since not everyone is willing to embark on such an unconventional way of living.

This site is a wonderful tool for anyone looking to research shipping container homes.

Anthony Hofman

Chapter 6

Alternative Ways To Use Shipping Containers

Aside from using your shipping container as a place of residence, there are hundreds of other ways to utilize this empty space. This of it as a canvas, you are free to let your imagination run wild with ideas - and that's what people have done. Everywhere, all around the world, people are using shipping containers for a wide variety of uses aside from storage and home residences. On a website known as Cube Depot, they list seventeen different ways to utilize a storage unit.

According to Cube Depot, people have created barn houses out of shipping containers because of their ability to withstand different types of inclement weather while maintaining the integrity of the structure and protecting the contents inside the storage unit. These barn houses measurements are also favorable to create a storage space for animals, yard tools and so much more. It is incredible the versatility that this space will give you.

Shipping container beach houses are another option for someone not looking to live in a container year-round. A lot of people cannot afford to purchase a home that costs over 600K, just to be on the beach. People would much rather purchase or rent a plot of land and build their own shipping container home on the land, thus creating their own affordable beach house. Also, due to the fact that shipping containers hold up well during inclement weather and hurricanes, living on the coast will not come with as many risks as modern homes would although you will still be subject to land fees and taxing.

Using a shipping container as a free standing deck or as a deck attachment is a great idea as well. Using the inside as a covered deck and the roof as an open deck, you are creating an affordable and functional, two story leisure unit for your home. You can also put in large windows or sliding doors to open the space up and give it a real open feel.

Cube Depot also states that you can easily make an "adjustable pop up container shop." With this shop, you can create a place of business whether it be retail, service or food related. According to Cube Depot, "a custom container project is perfect for pop-up food trucks or other types of businesses that sell their items on the streets. You can style your shipping containers using sliding or adjustable doors to fit your desired shop, making your business that more unique. A simplistic but intricate design expresses the originality of what container architecture holds."

Do not think it can be done? Cube Depot features a container that was designed by Adam Kalkin and Illy in 2007. Located in Venice, Italy, "This innovative shipping container cafe expresses the connection to beauty through art and design and is operated by four motors that open and lower the sides of the container. Lowering the sides of the container provides more space and enhances the experience. The container space includes a living room, a kitchen that is surrounded by a bedroom and bath, a dining area, and a library in the center."

Another interesting idea for shipping containers is making schools out of them. According to Cube Depot, these containers make great emergency shelters for tornadoes and other types of disaster relief. An article on Cube Depot also lays out ideas about making furniture from smaller containers. If you want to create something unique, while maintaining sound structure and durability, making a table and chair set, or coffee table out of old containers will add a practical yet artsy touch to any living space.

Another great idea the whole family – or even the whole neighborhood – will enjoy is creating a swimming pool out of old shipping containers. With the basic shape, you can use one or multiple containers to fit your space and needs. With lengths ranging from 10 feet to 53 feet, you can combine multiple containers to create different shapes or depths as you desire. You can also paint the containers any way you want, which can give some real artistic personal touches to your yard. With only minor construction needed to make adjustments for the filtration system, a shipping container can be a great starting point for a swimming pool.

You can also use a shipping container to create a patio or enclosed porch in your own backyard. You can cut out spaces for windows or doors so that you can enjoy your personal space all year-round.

Another idea is to transform a shipping container into a portable living space, like a camper. You'll have the freedom to travel with all the amenities of home. You'll save money by not needing to rent hotel rooms, since most campground rates are only a few dollars per night, or even cheaper when you stay at a weekly rate.

Another option is to customize a container that you can turn into a playroom for your children. They can be as loud as they want to without disrupting the inside of your home, and it is a great place for them to work on arts and crafts without the accidental spilling of paint or glitter on your living room carpet. You can turn the container into a movie theater, with sofas or cushions and blankets, where they can have movie nights with their friends – all while not disrupting your own plans to stay at home for the night. Letting your kids play outside and release all their energy is great for them, but even better for you! And you can size your container and configure it in a way that's perfect for your backyard.

Do you have deer, rabbits or other animals munching on your garden vegetables that you've so lovingly grown all summer long? The different sizes of available containers will allow you to get one that will be suitable for the plants you want to grow. Anything from a grapevine structure along the side, to fruit trees to corn to ornamental and aromatic lilac bushes, the possibilities really are endless. You can cut out windows and add some adjustable shades so you can vary the light that comes in by the different plants and areas they're in within the container. By using a shipping container to contain your garden, not only will you be able to protect it from animals, but you will be able to control the weeds that are bound to pop up in a traditional outdoor garden.

In Ariel Sharon National Park, located in Tel-Aviv, Israel, the bridge leading into the park is a 525-foot long bridge created entirely out of reused shipping containers in one continuous line, called the Eco-friendly Ecotainer Bridge. The park was once a landfill, converted now into a lush green park where the people of Tel-Aviv can escape the city life and all the noises and smells that come with city dwelling. The park and the bridge showcase the creativity that can be applied to utilizing objects and materials that most would consider just throwing away or letting go to waste.

London also features an area called Container City, a housing development made entirely out of used shipping containers. It is cost-effective to build and durable. The containers are stacked five-high and contain studios, lofts, and apartments.

Nicholas Lacey and Buro Happold are the architects that designed Container City, but the original idea came from Urban Space Management, a leader in innovative, creative, and attractive retail endeavors in London. Urban Space Management's mission statement revolves around three main principles:

1. Tread lightly upon the earth

2. Be Site-specific, cost-effective, and timely

3. Listen to the wants of the people, the place, and leave room for creativity.

Container City follows all of these guidelines and has been a jumping point for other container-based projects in London. Some of these include Necropolis Waterloo, Portishead Quays, BBC Broadcasting Studios, Islington Boxing Club, and many other projects in the city.

Steven Beese of RE:BE Design in New Orleans, Louisiana, has created a masterpiece for the New Orleans Voodoo Music and Art Festival. Known for its unconventionality, it made sense to create a space out of unconventional materials – shipping containers. In 2009, the festival committee repurposed six 40-foot containers and modified them to create a VIP lounge on the upper deck, and storage space below. The base, which is used for storage space during the festival's off-season, is comprised of four containers, which also contains a lounge and bar for patrons during the festival. The two containers that sit atop the base has been modified into a balcony for onlookers to enjoy the festival from above the street. To add to the funky appeal of the festival, the base has the word "VOODOO" outlined with perforated cutouts where patrons can view the festival outside while enjoying the luxuries inside the container lounge.

In Texas, there may be the most eco-friendly shipping container home ever created. Developed by Numen Development, L.P. and designed by Christopher Robertson, the Cordell House features numerous "green" elements, beginning with the construction itself, producing only twelve contractor bags of waste. It is also known for its energy-efficient design while displaying modern innovation and creativity. The home is constructed out of four shipping containers, with bamboo floors and low-VOC paints used throughout. Non-toxic insulation, combined with a white roof and glazing contributes to its passive solar design. The property even features a driveway made of 25 percent granite and 75 percent recycled glass.

A Mini-Farmery, sponsored by the well-known company Burt's Bees, is an eco-friendly "pop-up" on the American Tobacco Campus in Durham that features living walls and natural aesthetic beauty. The building is made from a reused 20-foot shipping container with other greenhouse components added. The roof of the container is used to grow flowers, sweet potatoes, and tomatoes, while inside they grow mushrooms, and the interior wall panels grow herbs and other greens. This mini version is Ben Greene's concept of an innovative agricultural project. He plans to create a full-scale Farmery made from a 45-foot shipping container with two levels, where an indoor organic farm will function on the upper level, and there will be a market on the lower level to sell the produce grown upstairs.

Wikipedia is a huge advocate for using shipping containers for more than two uses. Due to its informative nature, Wikipedia lays out a bunch of different ways in which you can use your shipping container aside from storage and a home. Wikipedia states, "Many structures based on shipping containers have already been constructed, and their uses, sizes, locations, and appearances vary widely."

The author of *How Buildings Learn*, Stewart Brand, needed an office to assemble all the materials he needed to write the book. He used an old shipping container, converted it into an office space, and documented the entire process in the book he was writing.

Architect Peter DeMaria of Southern California designed the first two-story home made from a shipping container in 2006. This structure was approved by the nationally recognized Uniform Building Code (UBC), following its strict guidelines for suitable dwellings. This home became known as the Redondo Beach House, and was the inspiration for the creation of Logical Homes. This company produces pre-fabricated container homes. In 2007, the Logical Homes created their leading project for the Computer Electronics show, in Las Vegas, known as the Aegean. .

In 2006, the Dutch company Tempohousing finished in Amsterdam the biggest container village in the world: 1,000 student homes from modified shipping containers from China.

A Dutch company called Tempohousing built the world's largest shipping container village in Amsterdam in 2006. Using containers sourced from China, it created 1000 rooms for student housing.

Standard ISO shipping containers, since 2002, have been used as self-contained on-site water treatment tanks, creating a cost-effective and modular solution for water treatment facilities and alleviating the need for total construction of a new building for housing water treatment systems.

During an MBA program field trip in the 2000s to Ciudad Juárez, Mexico, student Brian McCarthy was exposed to the poor neighborhoods of the city. This caused him to create prototypes for housing structures for the factory workers in Mexico.

In the United Kingdom, containers filled with sand were used to construct walls which are used like sandbags in electricity substations. This provides protection from flying debris from exploding insulators.

In Europe sits a 170-acre organized shopping mall made of alleys created by stacked shipping containers. This market is located in Odessa, Ukraine between the airport and central city, called Tolchok. It is also officially known as the Seventh-Kilometer Market with 16,000 vendors, employing 1200 security guards and maintenance workers.

In Bishkek, Kyrgyzstan, the Dordoy Bazaar is another market of comparable size to Tolchok. It is built almost completely out of shipping containers. It is popular with travelers from Russia Kazakhstan and known for its inexpensive merchandise and knock-off designer goods.

In 2011, a shopping mall in Christchurch, New Zealand that had previously been destroyed by an earthquake that struck the business district reopened but this time it was built out of shipping containers. Starbucks Coffee has also built a store using shipping containers (6350 N. Broadway, Chicago, IL 60660 USA).

Shipping containers have also been used for:

- Press boxes

- Hurricane shelters for horses and other animals

- Concession stands

- Affordable housing structures

- Fire and military training facilities

- School annexes

- Office space on construction sites

- Emergency shelters for natural disaster zones

- Studios for artists

- Moveable exhibition spaces

- Bank vaults

- Pop-up medical clinics

- Recording studios

- Radar stations

- Modular data centers

- Laboratories

- Temporary containment for combative inmates or criminals

- Bathrooms and showers for outdoor events

- Hotels

- Elevator and stairwell shafts

- Workshops

- Housing foundations in active seismic zones

- Roadblocks and blockades in hostile areas where protesting and rioting are frequent

- Accommodations at mining sites

- Aviation maintenance facilities for the US Marine Corps

- Hydroponic farms

- Food truck

- RVs/campers

On November 3, 1987, Phillip C. Clark applied for a patent which was granted to him on August 8, 1989, number 4854094, for what was described as a "method for converting one or more steel shipping containers into a habitable building at a building site and the product thereof." This documentation provides some of the earliest known plans for using shipping containers as a habitable space using basic architectural ideas. Even though he was granted the patent, the times showed no demand for such structures as this was a rather novel idea at the time he was requesting the patent. On the set of the film *Space Rage Breakout on Prison Planet* in 1985, Paul Sawyers described the extensive use of buildings made from shipping containers for various purposes. Even before this, in 1977, the US military explored the idea of using 20-foot shipping containers in a reported titled "Shipping Containers as Structural Systems."

During the Gulf War in 1991, the military used shipping containers in multiple nonstandard methods such as makeshift shelters and, with holes cut in the sides for ventilation, the transport of Iraqi prisoners of war. To this day the military continues to use shipping containers for shelters, often being reinforced with sandbags against interior walls to protect against weapons like rocket-propelled grenades (RPGs).

The recent abundance of shipping containers in North America is due to the decline of manufactured goods leaving North America over the last couple of decades. Most merchandise is now being mostly imported from Asia or Europe in containers that have to be shipped back empty, also called deadhead, which is extremely expensive. Rather than shipping old containers back, it is cheaper to buy new containers from Asia to pack goods in to be shipped to North America on a one-way journey.

This has become the reason for the green movement to reuse these containers in ways that, in the past, may have seemed unconventional. The more of a stockpile North America acquires, the cheaper and more readily available they will become for people who want to design their own shipping container homes or offices. Peter DeMaria recognized the trade imbalance with other countries, as has stated that "millions of containers are left in our ports every year."

As stated earlier in the list, even Starbucks has used shipping containers to create a unique storefront for their customers, focused on the aspect of recycling and thinking "outside the box." Alan Hilowilz, owner of the shipping container Starbucks states that "Our store designs reflect Starbucks' core mission as a gathering place for the communities we serve, as well as a commitment to reduce our environmental footprint and use our scale for good. Our designers were inspired to create this store both as a result of the shipyard that can be seen out the back windows of our headquarters in South Seattle, as well as a desire to recycle the same kind of shipping containers that transport our coffees and teas around the world."

Anthony Hofman

Chapter 7

Planning And Designing Your Shipping Container Home

When it comes to designing and planning your home, it can become overwhelming. This is even more so the case when you are dealing with a unique and unconventional space such as the shipping container homes. These homes restrict the amount of designs you can use because of their rectangular shape, requiring you make the most of the little space that you have after all your necessities are installed.

According to the Shipping Container Homes website, "If you do want to move forward with a shipping container home, you have several options. One is to look for a builder that offers prefabricated container homes. Shipping container home builders can be found online, and often their expertise is invaluable. Another is to go for container home plans or kits you can customize with specific options tailored to your specific needs. Whatever option you choose, be sure to research the company, builder or architect." It also stresses that you should look for references or customer reviews about the companies that are out there, not only for the quality of work, but to get an idea of how close to the customer's budgeted goals companies were able to reach. Many companies will low-ball estimates out of the gate to garner business, only to tack on additional costs once a customer signs a contract.

Even with the traditional home building process, there are permits and approvals that need to be secured to construct any kind of building. Many contractors that specialize in fabricating container homes have pre-planned designs available, and they are typically familiar with the work that goes into securing your permits, even with varying locations. Add to that the fact that you are using a shipping container, and the documentation process just grows. Experienced storage container builders will already be anticipating the bureaucratic process and will serve as a conduit between you and government agencies.

Planning anything can easily overwhelm even the most organized person. One of the best things you can do for yourself is to stay organized to keep your thoughts collected. Use a binder to keep out designs you like, different appliances and other fixtures that you want to incorporate in your home. With every decision you make, keep the receipt and any warranty or guarantee that comes with the product. It may seem foolish but in the long run, keeping these items can save you a lot of money in the future.

Keep business cards of any contractors that you use because should anything need to be fixed in the future, you may be able to contact people who previously did the work. Not only could this lead to discounts on the labor, but it could also be easier for the contractors because the work will be familiar to them. Keep a printout or log of any regulations and licenses that you are required to keep up to date on for your storage unit. Some places require different types of fines and fees in order to allow them to reside on the property, even if you own the property.

Keeping a record of all of these paid fines will keep you in good standing should anyone come and question you. You want to make sure everything you could ever need is easily accessible and in one place – preferably in a binder with sheet protectors to protect from light, weather, and water damage.

In order to plan and design your homes and your rooms, you need to know the dimensions of you home. Before you get your storage container you obviously will not know the exact dimensions, however this information and these measurements provided to you by Shipping Container Housing give you the general measurements for the most common storage containers and the rooms associated with them. According to Shipping

Container Housing, you do not want to live in a house that forces you to crawl around from room to room, nor do you need a house that is so huge you need a maintenance staff just to vacuum the carpets. The larger the home, the higher the costs will be – from construction and materials to tax bills and insurance. Usually one large or two moderately sized containers suit most customers just fine. However, depending on your family size or the purposes you intend to use your container home for (natural disaster shelter for the entire block, for example), you may want to choose to use three or four shipping containers to find the right size.

Below you will find dimensions for the most common types of shipping containers. The dimensions given are based on the frame of the container. Also included you will find the details on the available capacity of each container. Even the smallest containers are quite sizable when it comes to considering it for a living area.

Shipping Container Standard Dimensions – 20-Foot-Long Shipping Container (based on a length of 8 feet wide and 8.5 feet tall)

Cubic capacity: 1,165 cu. ft.

Interior square footage: approx. 133 sq. ft.

Half-height storage container dimensions that measure 20 feet long are 8 feet wide and 4.25 feet high.

Cubic capacity: 402 cu. ft.

Interior square footage: approx. 133 sq. ft.

Shipping Container Standard Dimensions - 40-Foot-Long Shipping Container

There are two options for a 40-foot container. Standard and high cube (HC) both measure 8 feet wide. The standard version is 8.5 feet high; the HC version is 9.5 feet high.

Cubic capacity of the standard: 2,350 cu. ft.

Cubic capacity of HC: 2,694 cu. ft.

Interior square footage: 273 sq. ft.

45, 48 and 53-Foot-Long Standard Shipping Container Dimensions

Containers that measure 45, 48 and 53 feet long are available in high cube varieties, which is 1 foot higher than the standard cube. All three varieties are 8 feet wide and 9.5 feet high.

45-Foot-Long Container

45-foot cubic capacity: 3,043 cu. ft.

Interior square footage: approx. 308 sq. ft.

53-foot shipping container

48-Foot-Long Container

48-foot cubic capacity: 3,454 cu. ft.

Interior square footage: approx. 376 sq. ft.

53-Foot-Long Containers

53-foot cubic capacity: 3,857 cu. ft.

Interior square footage: approx. 416 sq. ft.

To get a good feel for the size and number of containers you'd need to create your ideal space, you can compare the standard shipping container dimensions with the average dimensions of some the most common room types.

Remember that the size of a room needs to accommodate the room's functions as well as the furniture and other items that plan to fit into it. While you may have to adjust your room sizes to suit your exact furnishings and needs, you can spot check the typical room sizes to use as a guide when choosing the dimensions of a shipping container.

Living Room/Family Room

Small: 12' x 18' = 216 sq. ft.

Medium: 16' x 20' = 320 sq. ft.

Large: 22' x 28' = 616 sq. ft.

Dining Room

Small: 10' x 12' = 120 sq. ft.

Medium: 12' x 16' = 192 sq. ft.

Large: 14' x 18' = 252 sq. ft.

Kitchen

Small: 5' x 10' = 50 sq. ft.

Medium: 10' x 16' = 160 sq. ft.

Large: 12' x 20' = 240 sq. ft.

Kitchen Eating Area

Small: 10' x 10' = 100 sq. ft.

Medium: 12' x 12' = 144 sq. ft.

Large: 16' x 16' = 256 sq. ft.

Home Office

Small: 8' x 10' = 80 sq. ft.

Medium: 12' x 14' = 168 sq. ft.

Large: 14' x 18' = 252 sq. ft.

Bedroom

Small: 10' x 10' = 100 sq. ft.

Medium: 12' x 12' = 144 sq. ft.

Large: 14' x 16' = 224 sq. ft.

Bathroom

Small: 6' x 9' = 54 sq. ft.

Medium: 8' x 12' = 96 sq. ft.

Large: 10' x 16' = 160 sq. ft.

Pantry, Closets, Storage Areas

Small: 2' x 2'= 4 sq. ft.

Medium: 3' x 4' = 12 sq. ft.

Large: 4' x 6' = 24 sq. ft.

Also account for any foyer space, hallways and any additional function, furnishings or utilities that may need their own area, such the washer and dryer.

Dimension Consideration:

A few other considerations can come into play when you are examining the standard shipping container dimensions and planning your container home.

Ceiling Height:

If you want the standard 8-foot ceiling height, you are going to want a high cube container. The interior height of high cube containers is 8 feet 10 inches, giving you a full 10 inches of space for your HVAC, wiring and other connections you need to install above the finished ceiling. The standard shipping container dimensions are 7 feet 10 inches high in the interior, which would leave you with 7-foot ceilings after you installed your connections. High cubes are typically preferred for container housing.

Interior Space:

The same way HVAC and electrical accoutrements may eat up some ceiling space, your interior shipping container standard dimensions may lose some space due to insulation, wiring and other items you need to install in the walls. Even if the loss is minimal, and even though the dimensions of shipping containers are sizable, any loss of space can impact the overall feel of your container house interior.

Enclosures (or Lack Thereof):

Even though the containers may come as a fully enclosed unit, you certainly do not need to keep them that way. You can install plenty of windows, skylights, large, rolling doors or even leave an open space for al fresco dining or entertainment. You can also make use of the roof as a patio or garden area.

Creative Combinations:

Placing two containers side-by-side automatically doubles your space, but you do not have to stick with a boxy, symmetrical look. Container homes have been created with top floors that jut out above bottom floors, creating a shady overhang.

You can also play around with different heights by stacking containers on top of each other. Even if you start with a container or two as the base of your home, you are also free to build on using traditional building techniques combined with a solid foundation of shipping containers.

Additional Shipping Container Dimensions:

Not all shipping containers are fit for use with ship container homes but we are including dimensional information on these types as well. While these cargo container types are typically not used in shipping container home construction, a creative designer might have a use for them when designing a modern container home.

40' Open Top Container

Ratings

Maximum Gross Weight: 67,200 lbs.

Tare Weight: 8,640 lbs.

Payload: 58,557 lbs.

Capacity: 2,260 cu. ft.

Internal Open Top Container Dimensions

Length: 39' 1"

Length (between top headers): 38' 4"

Length (between corner gussets): 37' 5"

Width: 7' 6"

Width (between top rails): 7' 3"

Height: 7' 8"

Height (under top rail): 6' 5"

External Open Top Container Dimensions

Length: 40'

Width: 8'

Height: 8' 6"

Door Opening

Width: 7' 6"

Height: 7' 4"

20' Open Top Container

Ratings

Maximum Gross Weight: 67,200 lbs.

Tare Weight: 5,070 lbs.

Payload: 62,129 lbs.

Capacity: 1,164 cu. ft.

Internal Open Top Container Dimensions

Length: 19' 2"

Length (between top headers): 18' 5"

Length (between corner gussets): 17' 7"

Width: 7' 6"

Width (between top rails): 7' 3"

Height: 7' 6"

Height (under top rail): 7' 3"

External Open Top Container Dimensions

Length: 19' 10"

Width: 8'

Height: 8' 6"

Door Opening

Width: 7' 6"

Height: 7' 4"

40' Reefer Container

Ratings

Maximum Gross Weight: 71,650 lbs.

Tare Weight: 10,846 lbs.

Payload: 60,803 lbs.

Capacity: 1,942 cu. ft.

Internal Reefer Container Dimensions

Length: 37' 11"

Width: 7' 6"

Height: 7' 3"

Lashings/Bottom Rail: 6 pieces/side

Loading Line (height): 7' 2"

External Reefer Container Dimensions

Length: 40'

Width: 8'

Height: 8' 6"

Door Opening

Width: 7' 5"

Height: 7' 4"

20' Reefer Container

Ratings

Maximum Gross Weight: 67,200 lbs.

Tare Weight: 6,610 lbs.

Payload: 60,590 lbs.

Capacity: 950 cu. ft.

Internal Dimensions

Length: 17' 10"

Width: 7' 6"

Height: 7' 5"

Lashings/Bottom Rail: 4 pieces/side

Loading Line (height): 7' 2"

External Dimensions

Length: 19' 10"

Width: 8'

Height: 8' 6"

Door Opening

Width: 7' 5"

Height: 7' 4"

40' High Cube Reefer Container

Ratings

Maximum Gross Weight: 74,960 lbs.

Tare Weight: 10,120 lbs.

Payload: 64,840 lbs.

Capacity: 2,325 cu. ft.

Internal Dimensions

Length: 37' 11"

Width: 7' 5"

Height: 8' 4"

Lashings/Bottom Rail: 6 pieces/side

Loading Line (height): 8'

External Dimensions

Length: 40'

Width: 8'

Height: 9' 6"

Door Opening

Width: 7' 5"

Height: 8' 6"

40' Platform

Payload: 86,000 lbs.

Internal Dimensions

Length: 40'

Width: 8'

40' Flat Rack Container

Ratings

Maximum Gross Weight: 99,212 lbs.

Tare Weight: 10,803 lbs.

Payload: 88,409 lbs.

Concentrated Load Over Center 2 Meter Span: 56,000 lbs.

Internal Shipping Container Standard Dimensions

Length (between end panels): 39' 6"

Length (between corner posts): 38' 3"

Width (over bottom side rail): 7' 2"

Width (between corner posts): 7' 7"

Height (side rail to top casting): 6' 4"

External Shipping Container Standard Dimensions

Length: 40'

Width: 8'

Height: 8' 6"

20' Flat Rack Container

<u>Ratings</u>

Maximum Gross Weight: 74,950 lbs.

Tare Weight: 6,040 lbs.

Payload: 68,819 lbs.

Concentrated Load Over Center 2 Meter Span: 44,094 lbs.

<u>Internal Dimensions</u>

Length (between end panels): 19' 6"

Length (between corner posts): 18' 2"

Width (over bottom side rail): 7' 2"

Width (between corner posts): 7' 3"

Height (side rail to top casting): 7' 2"

20' Open Rack Container.

External Dimensions

Length: 19' 10"

Width: 8'

Height: 8' 6"

40' Collapsible Flat Rack

<u>Ratings</u>

Maximum Gross Weight: 99,212 lbs.

Tare Weight: 10,803 lbs.

Payload: 88,409 lbs.

Concentrated Load Over Center 2 Meter Span: 56,000 lbs.

<u>Internal Dimensions</u>

Length (between end panels): 39' 6"

Length (between corner posts): 38' 3"

Width (over bottom side rail): 7' 2"

Width (between corner posts): 7' 7"

Height (side rail to top casting): 6' 4"

<u>External Dimensions</u>

Length: 40'

Width: 8'

Height: 8' 6"

Collapsible Height: 2' 1

20' Tank Container

Payload: 6,764 lbs.

Capacity: 904 cu. ft.

Internal Dimensions

Length: 20'

Width: 8'

Height: 8' 6"

Container Dimension Metric Conversions

When we talk about shipping container standard dimensions, we can use the following conversions:

10 feet = 2 991 mm

20 feet = 6 058 mm

30 feet = 9 125 mm

40 feet = 12 192 mm

45 feet = 13 716 mm

The current widths are:

8feet = 2 438 mm

8.6 feet = 2 590.8 mm"

Having these general measurements will not only help you plan out and design the layout of your storage unit, but will also allow you to decide how much room you think you will need in comparison to what you have now. Take measurements of furniture pieces that you absolutely cannot part with and use those to gauge what type of space you will need.

Anthony Hofman

Chapter 8

Quotes From Supporters And Other Resourceful Individuals

Using a shipping container as a home can be a form of resourcefulness and even a form a recycling. When you think of someone living in a shipping container, you do not often think about middle aged, baby boomer generation used to the white picket fence and the 9-5 jobs.

"If you are the type of person who has to fulfill your dreams, you've gotta be resourceful to make sure you can do it. I came out to California when I was 21, thinking my New York credentials would take me all the way. I came back home a year later all dejected and a failure. "Vin Diesel

"Much of the Netherlands lies considerably below sea level, as you well know. Through the process of building dikes to wall out the salty sea and through pumping the water into canals, the country of the ingenious, resourceful, and doughty Dutch has literally been born of the sea." Joseph B. Wirthlin

"It is not that bad things never happen. But there's a pattern in which most people are calm, resourceful, altruistic, and they improvise emergency systems that work really well - whether it is getting the babies out of a collapsed hospital or putting together a community kitchen to feed everybody for the next few months." Rebecca Solnit

"Jane was my wicked stepmother: she was generous, affectionate and resourceful; she salvaged my schooling and I owe her an unknowable debt for that. One flaw: sometimes, early on, she would tell me things designed to make me think less of my mother, and I would wave her away, saying, 'Jane, this just backfires and makes me think less of you." Martin Amis

"Life's too short to hang out with people who are not resourceful." Jeff Bezos

"Modern science, then, so far from being an enemy of romance, is seen on every hand to be its sympathetic and resourceful friend, its swift and irresistible helper in its serious need, and an indulgent minister to its lighter fancies." Richard Le Gallienne

"Dear Mr. Schneider, I attended your elementary

School almost thirty years ago

And I'm very sure that

You will remember

Me.

My name is Suzy.

I'm that hyperactive girl

From the Egyptian family

Who used to always play dead

On the playground during

Recess.

You used to keep me

After school a lot,

And then my father would

Force me to make the long

Walk home in the cold or rain.

Sometimes I would arrive

After dark.

I'm writing to tell you

That I was bored as a kid.

I was bored by your curriculum

And the way I was always taught a

Bunch of useless

Junk.

I did not like being locked up

In a prison of scheduled time

Learning about irrelevant material,

And watching belittling cartoons and

Shows approved by academia that

Made me even more

Bored.

As a kid

Who was constantly

Growing, evolving, and

Being shaped by all around me,

I wanted to travel,

See other kids

In the world like me,

To understand what was going

On amongst us and around us,

To know what we were here for

And what was our real purpose

For existence.

I have some questions

I would like to ask you, Mr. Schneider,

Now that I know that you are no

Longer a school principal,

But the new superintendent

Of the entire school

District.

I want to know

Why racism today

Was not clearly explained to me

Even though we covered events

That happened long ago.

I want to know why you

Never shared with us

Why other countries

Never liked us,

Why we are taught to compete,

To be divided in teams,

And why conformity is associated

With popularity, while

Eccentricity is considered

Undesirable?

I want to know

Why my cafeteria lunches

Were slammed packed

With bottom-tier

Processed junk food

Only suitable

For pigs?

And why is it

That whenever a bully

Slammed a kid into a locker for

His lunch money,

Nobody explained to us

That egotism, selfishness and greed

Were the seeds of

War?

I want to know

Why we were never taught

To stick up for each other,

To love one another, and that

Segregation sorted by the

Occupations of our fathers,

The neighborhoods we lived in, our houses,

Choices of sport, wealth, clothing,

Anthony Hofman

Color of our skin

And the texture of our hair

Should never, ever

Divide us?

And lastly,

I want to know why

Is it that whenever I pledged

Allegiance to the flag,

I was never told that I was

Actually hailing to the

Chief?

You used to say that

I was a troubled child,

A misfit, and that I needed

Obedience training,

But you never acknowledged that

I was the fastest runner in the district

And that I took the school

To State and Nationals to compete

In the Spelling Bee among kids

Grades higher than me.

And that it was me,

Who won that big trophy

That sat in your office when you

Used to detain me for hours

And tell me I was no

Good.

Mr. Schneider,

If we are not taught truths as kids,

Then how do you expect us to

Grow up to be truthful citizens?

If we are only being taught the written way,

And it has not shown positive effects

In societies of yesterday or today,

Then how can we progress as a

United and compassionate

Nation?

What good is it,

To memorize the histories

Of our forefathers,

Without learning what could be

Gained from their lessons and mistakes

To improve our future

Tomorrows?

And finally,

I want to thank you;

For I know you have a tough job

Dealing with rebellious children like me.

Your job of mass processing and boxing

The young minds of America has not been an easy one,

And I congratulate you

On your recent promotion.

But I sincerely want to thank you,

Thank you,

And thank you,

For always pointing out

That I was

Different."

— Suzy Kassem, Rise Up and Salute the Sun: The Writings of Suzy Kassem

"To choose not to be part of a team or religion does not make me non-religious; for my religion is Truth and I am very much in love with God. I do not need to align myself with a specific messenger if I already understand God's message. And the way I think is not considered 'New Age', since common sense is not new. So long as you act and speak with love and truth in you, and are good to your fellow man — in that you treat everybody as you would want yourself to be treated, your heart will stand by God regardless of the label you have assigned to your mind."

— Suzy Kassem

"You are not a one-dimensional human being. You are not your social media etiquette, a picture, a few things said under stress or through misunderstanding. You are much more. You are a fearless and wonderful soul who loves greatly. The people that matter are the ones that see all the dimensions of your soul, not just the superficial. They will climb inside that box with you not because they are not sure if they will ever find your uniqueness in another person. They do so because they feel safe enough to share their uniqueness with you. They see your faults and know that they have them also. They feel the walls lowered and the freedom of being themselves. Honesty is never guarded or regretted. That is what makes that box home."

— Shannon L. Alder

"About Differences: Those who would believe in a higher power by whatever name must also believe that same higher power made all things. On that basis, people of good character will recognize that some people are different from ourselves, in color, gender, speech, opinion, lifestyle, and in other ways. Different is not an evaluation. As I taught my children while they were growing up, "Different is only different." Celebrate differences for therein lies the basis for much of what we learn in life."

— James Osborne

"Bravery in a fictional character is one thing--it is easy to imagine and easy to write. Bravery in real life offers many challenges. We want to believe we will be brave if a situation requires us to. But if we over-think it, we will certainly fail. One simply needs to act toward the best possible result rather than to ponder all of the possibilities."

— Susan Wingate, *The Deer Effect*

"It has always been simple, but making it hard was always your way of avoiding pain. If you want to change your life, you have to change what you are doing. It wasn't his fault, her fault, their fault or the circumstances. It was your inability to choose. So, life chose for you. Somewhere in that crazy mind of yours time stopped. You thought someone would rescue you, but they did not. You have to rescue yourself. This is not a fire you can put out; you have to walk through it, in order to reach life. Getting burned is a part of growth, did not you know?"

— Shannon L. Alder

"Two roads diverged in a yellow wood, but I chose neither one. Instead, I set sail in my little boat to watch a sunset from a different view that could not be seen from shore. Then I climbed the tallest mountain peak to watch the amber sun through the clouds. Finally, I traveled to the darkest part of the valley to see the last glimmering rays of light through the misty fog. It was every perspective I experienced on my journey that left the leaves trodden black, and that has made all the difference."

— Shannon L. Alder

"Do not be afraid to color outside the lines. Take risks and do not be afraid to fail. Know that when the world knocks you down, the best revenge is to get up and continue forging ahead. Do not be afraid to be different or to stand up for what's right. Never quiet your voice to make someone else feel comfortable. No one remembers the person that fits in. It is the one who stands out that people will not be able to forget."

— Nancy Arroyo Ruffin

"You cannot put your heart into everything; you've just got to show up. And if your heart is worn all over you, then so be it, but you cannot pull it out of you and put it in places, or put it in people's hands. Because you are like this wild and quiet and laughing thing and people are like things that stand there and do not understand what's going on; so when you put your heart into things like that, you are going to feel either stupid, or very hurt, or both. And it is not people's faults that they are just standing there. I mean, you are the different one; they're not different; they're all the same."

— C. JoyBell C.

"It is been happening since I was in kindergarten. Not them all the time, but other kids, you know. Every day. It never stops, and it never goes away, thanks to the Internet--it just keeps happening every minute, every day. And I just want it to stop. I think about how to do it, you know. How to kill them. All kinds of elaborate things, like trapping them in pits and burying them alive, or covering them with concrete."

— Rachel Caine, *Bite Club*

"The blending, of course, is the challenge. Most creatures who are special cannot seem to stop themselves from announcing the fact, despite the dangers that come with being different from the rest of your species. If you tie a red string around a wren's leg, the others in the flock will peck it to death."

— Kim Wright, *City of Darkness*

"The person who follows the crowd will usually go no further than the crowd. The person who walks alone is likely to find himself in places no one has ever seen before."

— Albert Einstein

Anthony Hofman

Chapter 9

Recommendations

Because not everyone knows where to start when it comes to creating a home made from shipping containers, here are four different products that will be not only helpful in your quest for shipping container living but are also affordable.

Shipping containers are a relatively small space, depending on how many containers you are using. For the most part, people generally use one or two containers to make their home out of. Due to this small square footage, smart storage solutions are important to ensure you use your space wisely. A great product on Amazon for doing this is product by iWill Create Pro – a storage container in a variety of colors that is not only stylish but also incredibly functional. This storage container has dividers, different openings and comes in a perfect space saving size for only $28.99. These are cloth storage boxes meant for organizing that comes with removable dividers and lids. They also come in an array of colors to choose from.

Shipping containers are made of metal which means they will rust. Although rust is inevitable, you can prevent the spread and possibly reverse the effects early on if you treat your walls and surfaces that appear to be more susceptible to rust. This product on Amazon called "Rust Converter Ultra" and is a product that is packaged in a container similar to a bleach container. At $41.99 for one gallon, this product stops the spread of existing rust, prevents corrosion and rust from appearing in the future, forms a long lasting, protective shield, diminishes the need for sand blasting, scraping, or grinding, and can be applied by brushing or spraying. This product has a large customer review base with the average rating of four and a half stars out of five.

Due to the small space, Oak Leaf has created these sleek and attractive, adhesive wall hooks that can be placed on nearly any surface and stick. These hooks are waterproof and are made of heavy duty wood and stainless steel. The description of this product states that 6 hooks made of high quality 3M self-adhesive arrive included with the package. You can use these hooks on a wide variety of surfaces, such as finished walls, glass, wood and gypsum board.

The hanger itself is constructed of stainless steel and the backing is produced from high-quality bamboo. It is fortified by 3M adhesive which is known for its durability and strength. Each hook only weighs three ounces and measures 61mm wide by

41mm high, but it can hold up 4.5 pounds, showcasing that it may have the strongest adhesive available on the market.

Because of the natural look of the bamboo backing, it is a useful accessory that can also be somewhat decorative around the kitchen, bathroom, home, or office. The adhesive is tested to work on multiple surfaces including glass, wood, ceramic tile, painted surfaces and many others. Just make sure the surface has been cleaned and is dry and place the hook wherever you need it. A word of caution though – the adhesive is NOT REMOVABLE. Take some time to consider where you need your hook before placing on any surface. This product is priced at $9.99 for 6 hooks and has an average of four out of five stars as the rating.

Oak Leaf's mission statement is that they create OAK LEAF with a one objective in mind: to provide simplistic, low-cost, high quality products for all types of households. That means that they have a commitment of 100% satisfaction. They view themselves as customers also so they back their hooks by saying that if you have any problems at all to contact them for a full refund or return.

Finally, the fourth product we will go over is the folding screen by ACME. This product is great for small spaces because it divides a room without you having to build an entire wall – a feat that would prove difficult in a stainless steel storage unit. This screen is attractive and has colors that will match with nearly every pattern and color you choose for your home. The screen is 71 inches high with each panel measuring 18 inches wide. This screen is priced at $54.76 on sale, an incredible value for such an attractive and useful object. The screen has an average rating of four and a half out of five stars with one hundred and eight reviews on Amazon.

Chapter 10

Some Things To Keep In Mind When Constructing A Shipping Container Home

It is easy to see why shipping container homes have become so popular. The whole thing seems easy enough. All you need to do is buy the container or containers. They're pre-fabricated so one container can equal one room. You can stack the containers together, and you have multiple rooms. If you join two or more containers together, you have a larger room. Sounds simple enough, right?

Well, not really. There are plenty of factors to consider when using a shipping container or shipping containers to make a house. The first thing to keep in mind is that these were never really meant to be used for building; they are cargo containers, and they have been built for that. In addition, just having a container is not enough. You need to think about things such as an HVAC system, insulation and so on. It does not help either that since this is such an unusual type of home, you do not have too many experts handy to guide you and advise you.

Keeping all this in mind here are a few tips from experts in the field of shipping container homes. These are people who are either designers or owners of such homes, and the advice they have to give comes from the experience that they have gained building and designing these types of homes.

1. **See Before You Buy**

   This is the advice given by Larry Wade. The company you buy the containers from will reassure you, of course, that the containers you have bought are in good condition. But remember that shipping containers are used to transport all sorts of goods in all sorts of conditions ranging from bad roads to rough seas. While they are built to be durable enough to withstand these conditions, they are also going to 'beat all to heck' as Wade put it when he received his containers.

   When you stop to think about it, it really is good advice for buying just about anything. When it comes to shipping containers, therefore, consider this advice gold.

2. **Spend a Little Extra**

   While lamenting the state of the shipping containers he bought, Larry Wade also wished that he had spent just a bit extra. One-Trip containers are easily available and do not cost that much more than a used container. Most importantly, they're brand new, so you do not really have to worry about the condition of the container or containers that you buy. Having said that, the first tip still holds good. Always see what you are buying before you actually buy it.

3. Learn the Local Regulations

Of course, this depends on the size of the container you are using. But that again depends on what the minimum size to get a building permit is. Do you see what I mean? Every county is going to have its own rules and regulations. When you expand that to state and then to country, things become even more complicated.

You no longer have to worry about just council rules. There are different laws governing what is appropriate building material and what is not, who can build it and so on. Most importantly, you have to take into account different climates and weather patterns. What works in Chile, for example, will not necessarily work in Denmark and vice versa.

Determine where you want to locate your shipping container home and then research the local rules and regulations thoroughly so that you know what you can and cannot do, what permits you need to get and so on.

4. Find Someone to Take Care of All of It

It is important to find one person or company who can take you through the entire process, from start to finish. This means the person who gets, designs and modifies the exterior also takes care of the interior. Again this is something that makes sense when you think about it. The company that builds the shipping container home will know all about the structure of the home and can incorporate designs into the interior that not only complement the exterior but work with it on a structural basis.

This also means that you as the homeowner do not have to go through the headache of remembering stuff you had no idea you needed to remember.

Of course, the problem with this particular tip is that there are not that many people or companies who can do this for you. It will really depend on where you are located, what your budget is like and other such considerations.

5. Know the Shipping Container Market

Do a lot of research before you buy a shipping container or containers to construct your home. As I have mentioned in previous chapters, shipping containers come in a variety of sizes. Look up the various sizes and see what you need. Investigate the market thoroughly to know what is available and what is not. Do not just get the first thing that clears your head. Remember that you'll probably have to install an HVAC in addition to other fixtures that will dramatically reduce the clearing space. Consider all of this before you buy a container.

6. Understand the Structure of a Shipping Container

This is something that you cannot afford to forget. As I've said earlier, a shipping container is meant to do exactly that – ship stuff around. It is not meant for construction. The roof of a shipping container is fairly thin and dents quite easily. The walls of the container act as both braces and load bearers.

All this becomes very important when you consider that you will have to cut out portions of the walls of the containers to make doors and windows. The more portions you remove, the less load the walls can bear. Remove enough section and you'll find the whole thing collapsing about your head. It is simple physics.

You need to remember that for every piece you cut out from a wall, you need to compensate elsewhere.

7. Huge Savings Do Not Happen

Yes, shipping containers are relatively cheap. But think about it. Are you just going to get the container, put a few sticks of furniture in and start living in it?

You will need to get your containers reinforced, stacked, cut, insulated, prepared for plumbing and electricity and many other such basics. You will also need to install an HVAC system that will require even more cutting and modifications. All of this together can add up to a sum that is not significantly different from what you would have spent buying a house of the same size or with the same number of rooms.

In the end, modifying a shipping container to make it into your dream home can end up costing as much as the ordinary dream home would.

8. Minimize Welding

Since this is a metal box we are talking about, at some point in time, you will end up welding some parts of it. However, keep in mind that welding can be a pretty expensive proposition, not to mention the fact that it requires an expertise that you will probably not have. Another minus is that welding can take a long time. Therefore, try to keep the welding to a minimum when setting up your shipping container home. Of course, you may not have a choice about it, but if you do your research, you should be able to figure out how to manage it.

9. Know About the Insulation

A shipping container is made of steel. As such, it is an excellent conductor of heat and cold. If you live in a region with a colder climate, you could end up freezing in your home. Another problem with lower temperatures is condensation. Inside the warmth of your home, the colder air will condense and form droplets of water on the walls. In the long term, that translates into rust.

Do proper research on how to insulate your shipping container home adequately. Remember, not only do you have to worry about heat escaping, but you also need to make sure that your walls do not end up rusting.

10. What about the Plumbing?

This is one of those things we do not really think about. After all, when we are buying a home, plumbing is already there. We may have to look into the condition of the pipes and so on, but we do not really have to worry about getting the plumbing in, in the first place.

The same cannot be said of a shipping container. It is basically a rectangular box. You are going have to consult the designer and determine exactly where you want the plumbing and learn what kind of plumbing the container can handle. If you are planning to stack more than one shipping container for more rooms and a bigger building, you may want to have the plumbing chases cut out of the ceilings and floors so that the pipes can be run easily.

11. Thought about the Wind Yet?

You are basically talking about large sheets of corrugated steel here. When the wind blows, it is going to make the steel walls and sometimes even roof, vibrate. This can make for a pretty noisy home, especially if you live in an area that is wind prone.

Again, you need to do research here. First of all, find out whether the location where you are planning to construct your shipping container home does indeed get a lot of wind. Next, you need to find out what you can do to mitigate the effects of the wind. One good idea is to plant vegetation with heavy foliage so that it can screen off the wind and you can enjoy a quiet home.

As I'm sure you've noticed by now, one point that I keep repeating in many points is research. This is not a coincidence. When experts and shipping container homeowners were asked what they wished they had known before they started on this journey, the ones who had the least amount of problems were the ones who had researched the subject as thoroughly as possible. The thing is, this is a new type of housing. There are not that many people in your immediate vicinity who can give you reliable advice on this, unlike when you go to buy a conventional house. Therefore, to save yourself a lot of time, effort, and even money, it is a good idea that you first research this topic as completely as possible. Once you are armed with information, you'll find that it is much easier to get the whole thing done. But do remember that mistakes are inevitable, especially if you are doing it for the first time. You will need to plan for such contingencies. Doing adequate research will ensure that the mistakes you make are not serious and you can enjoy your shipping container home once it is completed, without any qualms.

Anthony Hofman

Chapter 11

How To Insulate Your Shipping Container Home

This one is very important. As I've discussed in previous chapters, shipping containers are made out of steel which is a very good conductor of heat and cold. This means that if you live in a very hot area, you might bake in the heat and if you live in a cold region, you could end up freezing. In addition, you also need to consider the effects of condensation on your home. Without adequate protection, you could end up with rust or mold in your home.

So, as has become clear, you need to have proper insulation. It might sound cheaper not to bother with insulation at all, but I can guarantee that the first hot day of summer or snowfall in winter will change your mind in a jiffy. Believe me, in the long run, it is more cost-effective to insulate your shipping container home than to leave it as it is.

Of course, all the insulation methods you may be considering will depend on one crucial factor – the climate. If you live in a cold region, you will need plenty of insulation not just to keep your home warm, but also to prevent condensation that could lead to rusting and mold. If, in addition to cold, you will also experience a lot of rainfall then you will need to use foam insulation so that the vapor does not get in.

On the other hand, if the climate you are living in is very hot and dry, you will not need as much insulation as you would in a cold climate. Whatever insulation you use will have to be designed around keeping your home as cool as possible.

So, without further ado, let us take a look at what insulation options you have, how to use them, and which option will suit which situation the best.

Foam Insulation

Spray foam insulation has a lot of advantages going for it. First of all, this is the fastest method of insulation. Secondly, the barrier it provides is seamless, which prevents rusting and mold from getting a toehold in your home. It provides the highest R rating, which is basically how well the foam can resist the heat flow. Spray foam can be sprayed into gaps as well, regardless of their size. It is extremely flexible.

The only problem with using spray foam insulation is that it can be on the expensive side. Also, it can end up being quite messy as compared to other insulation methods.

When applying spray foam, keep in mind that not only the interior and exterior walls of the containers but the space underneath the containers needs to be sprayed so that the moisture does not get in that way. The best and most effective spray foam insulation is the closed cell polyurethane foam.

To make the exterior walls look more attractive, you can paint the foam on the exterior walls once it has set.

Insulation Panels

Panel insulation needs stud walls to fit. For those of you who prefer the DIY approach, this is the best type of insulation. The panels are available in predefined sizes and can be fit into the gaps in the stud walling. Panel insulation is also quicker to fit than a similar insulation type known as blanket insulation. However, panel insulation can also be slightly more expensive.

The thing to remember here is that the panel insulation has a relatively small depth but a high insulating value. Therefore, if foam insulation is too expensive for you, you can look at panel insulation which comes at a comparatively moderate price and ensures that the thickness of your insulation is at a minimum.

Blanket Insulation

This one is again a good buy for the DIY enthusiasts, especially considering that this is the cheapest type of insulator that we discuss. Just as panel insulation does, blanket insulation also needs stud walls so it can be fitted in. It is a fast method since once the stud walls are up, you can fit the blanket insulation in the gaps quite fast. The most common blanket insulation is something known as rock wool, and it is mineral.

One thing that you need to keep in mind with this type of insulation is that it is sometimes made of fiberglass and therefore, needs to be handled with care. There is prescribed personal protective equipment that you will need to wear while installing this insulation. This gear includes safety glasses, gloves, dust mask and protective closing.

Since this is the cheapest type of insulation, if you are functioning on a tight budget, this one is probably your best bet.

Eco-friendly Insulation

Since one of the main reasons people want to live in shipping container homes is that these are sustainable and environmentally friendly, eco-friendly insulation becomes a good idea to take this idea forward. Some options here are wool, cotton, mud and even a living roof.

Wool

This one is quite similar to the blanket insulation that I discussed earlier. The material, though, is natural sheep wool instead of fiberglass, which can be quite controversial. This type of insulation does not have the kind of energy requirements that the fiberglass version does.

Cotton Insulation

Cotton insulation, like wool insulation, is a type of blanket insulation. It utilizes recycled clothes made of cotton. It is renewable and can be grown fast.

One thing to consider, though, is that cotton insulation is more expensive than the fiberglass version.

Living Roof

The first thing you need to know here is that this is not a direct substitute for regular insulation. However, it is very helpful in reducing the temperatures inside your home during the hot summer months. While during the rainy season, you will not experience any benefits from this roof, during the summer it can reduce temperatures by as much as eight percent.

In addition, this has the additional advantage of looking really different and cool.

Mud Walls

Mud is not only great as just an insulator, but it can also actually be used to build entire homes. Of course, that is not our focus here. Like the living roof, mud can be used to keep the heat out in climates that are dry and hot.

You can use the mud on the roof of the shipping container and also on the walls. When you apply the mud to the external walls, be sure to use battens which will help the mud to stick to the container.

Keep in mind, though, that if you live in a rainfall heavy area, mud is not a great idea. It will flow off in the first rain!

Conclusion

I hope that you found this book to be what you were looking for when it comes to an alternative type of home. You should now be aware of what shipping container homes are and how you can get one. We have also explored the advantages and disadvantages of this type of a home. Whatever you desire to call home, you have many options available to you since building a shipping container home is, at the most basic steps, exactly like building a traditional home to your own specifications.

Not only can they be used as a home, but they can also be used as nearly any type of building aside from the obvious. Whether you choose to create a swimming pool for your family, a giant container garden, or a kid's theater room, you will find that having that extra bit of space can be quite luxurious. Shipping containers may be a fad that burns out in the next decade, or it may take off and evolve into a whole new way of sustainable and eco-friendly living. Take this book with a grain of salt, the resources, websites, and quotes combined in this book create a priceless guide to learning about the residential shipping container industry.

In addition, we have looked at design ideas, how to insulate such a home and what you need to keep in mind before you set out to construct or have such a home constructed. Remember that appropriate and thorough research is your best friend in what is still a new field of home building. You also need to consider your specifications based on your area – if you live in a flood plain, it would not be wise to construct your home underground or without a proper foundation.

I hope that you enjoyed this book and that you took something useful from it. I will be very grateful if you choose to leave a review about this book. Thank you very much for purchasing this book.

References

Opinion: What's Wrong With Shipping Container Housing? Everything. *Arch Daily* Sept. 13, 2015. http://www.archdaily.com/773491/opinion-whats-wrong-with-shipping-container-housing-everything

Shipping containers offer welcome homes in Phoenix. *BigStory*. April 29, 2014. http://bigstory.ap.org/article/13ca87f00b89401690e08fa7f2be a2ab/shipping-containers-offer-welcome-homes-phoenix

Starbucks Opens Store Made From Recycled Shipping Containers. *Zdnet.* January 7, 2012. http://www.zdnet.com/article/starbucks-opens-store-made-from-recycled-shipping-containers/

Standard Shipping Container Dimensions. *Shipping Container Housing Guide.* October 11, 2016. http://www.shipping-container-housing.com/shipping-container-standard-dimensions.html

Anthony Hofman

Resourceful Quotes. *Brainy Quotes.* October 2, 2016. http://www.brainyquote.com/quotes/keywords/resourceful.html